Workday Catalyst

Proven Tips, Reminders and Inspiration to Advance and Inspire Your Career Journey

By Hope LeNoir

Copyright © 2019 by Hope LeNoir

All rights reserved. No part of this publication may be reproduced, distributed, or transmitted in any form or by any means, including photocopying, recording, or other electronic or mechanical methods, without the prior written permission of the publisher, except in the case of brief quotations embodied in critical reviews and certain other noncommercial uses permitted by copyright law. For permission requests, write to the publisher, addressed "Attention: Permissions Coordinator," at the address below.

Rise and Fly ©, LLC
800 East Lamar Blvd. Suite 173
Arlington, TX 76011
www.riseandfly.net

Ordering Information:
Quantity sales. Titles are available for bulk purchases for business, educational, fund raising or sales promotional use. For details, contact the publisher at the address above.

ISBN-9781703681918

INTRODUCTION

I wrote this book just for you. You have what it takes to journey beyond your wildest career ambitions. I know that for sure. You are a career catalyst to be reckoned with. Your skill, your drive, your purpose, continues to grow every day. Sometimes all we need is a little bit of encouragement, inspiration, a gentle push, and touch of insight before each workday in order to keep growing. This book does just that. I got you. Come on. Let's soar!

- Hope LeNoir

Got a *PLAN?*

Good. Now say it with me, "New Year, here I come!"

One of the greatest surprises about making a plan is no matter what, you'll end up somewhere. Your goal is to be further down the career path than you are now. No matter the time of year, take time to write down your plan. Even a simple one with three bullet points. Taking this action strengthens your commitment and activates your growth. Got your pencil ready?

Your Monday will not be like your Friday. Take the opportunity to **make the difference happen.**

Had a long week? Had an okay week? Take this opportunity to make next week better. No need to wait until the next Monday to *start over*. You can write your story now for a fantastic week. Focus on creating a better week one day at a time. Each day presents an occasion to make it a positively amazing day. How will you improve your week **today**? I can't wait to celebrate with you!

For crying out loud, just
say, "Thank you."

Saying thank you is one of the most rewarding and simple currencies to give and receive. It shows you recognize and appreciate the gift. Cultivating relationships based on mutual respect, appreciation, and genuine gratitude puts the right people in your corner in order to further your career endeavors. Thank-yous also set you up to pay it forward for others on their own career journeys.

To that end, what are you thankful for today? Who gave that to you? Have you told them thank you yet?

*I will **believe** in what you don't believe in.*

Strange huh? Billions of people have told you to believe in yourself. What if one day that's difficult for you? Guess what? I believe in you. I believe you are capable of living in and enjoying your career purpose. One day, you'll believe in that too, beyond measure. Start by boldly reaching out to your resources for help and tips. Seek feedback and listen to and appreciate those who believe in you. I am one of them. I believe in you. You've got this.

***Shhhh…Listen**, because sometimes you'll be prompted to stop.*

Yes, sometimes it's okay to stop. Listen to your intuition. Notice your surroundings. For example, what are your clients telling you? What is the market saying? What are your predictions of the future? What is your Higher Power instructing you to do? Does what you've heard from these areas line up? Aha! Listen carefully. It may be time to stop and reroute to meet your goal.

*There will be **disappointment** and pain.*

ALL successful men and women have gone through some sort of disappointment or pain. Sometimes before *and* after reaching the first mark. Don't ask yourself *why me*? Don't give up due to what feels like a million points of failure. Those are reasons to reevaluate a process, none of those are reasons you should give up on your career goals.

We have all had disappointments and pain, sometimes we reroute our journey, but we don't let disappointments stop our journey. We learn from them, adjust as necessary, and keep moving forward. Connect with your circle of strength and grow from the experience.

Don't stop your assignment.

Yes, your assignment. Assignment is the important word. It's your passion, your calling, that thing that doesn't feel like *work*. It's critical to know your purposed assignment. That means knowing what you've been assigned to do in your life. Once you discover this, embrace it and care for it. Don't stop what you've been assigned to do. There is where you will find great fulfillment and touch the lives of many others. Some seen. Some unseen.

*Most people **grow <u>up</u>**, and then they die?*

Ouch! That's not for you. Keep growing in your career. Don't die out. Aim to grow, then grow some more, then share your growth and leave a fantastic legacy of evolvement! Don't see an end and stop being magnificent. There is always another level to strive for, show out, and celebrate. Keep the journey going!

*You are **unusual**. You are **GREAT**.*

Aim to be unusual. Don't aim to be proficient at what everyone else is already doing—set yourself apart by not only doing something better, but also differently. Think about that today. How can you do things in a great way that is noticeably different than what your peers or leaders are doing today? How will you do **that** and do it consistently?

*Be alone. Really **alone**.*

Extreme Introvert or Energized Extravert, everyone needs a moment or two of alone time. You deserve it. Take this time to breathe, think, imagine, and celebrate everything about your career endeavors. What have you learned? What are you thankful for? What do you want more of? Where do you want to go? Make sure you are taking enough time to relax, reflect and rejuvenate.

*It's like food. If you don't have it for a while, you don't **crave for it** (as much).*

I see you! You're jazzed about what you've found out about your career drivers. You recognize your strengths. I've triggered your passion. You know what it is that you love. Don't let that go. Do something every day, big or small, that will nurture your career goals. Don't let it sit idle with the thought that you'll get back to it later. If you do that, you might just lose the drive.

It's like food. If you don't taste it for a while, you lose your craving for all its goodness, or you just might believe you don't need or want it anyway.

Manifest *love, kindness, forgiveness, service.*

Give it a try. Manifest love (knowing that love is an action, not a feeling). Be kind (knowing that kindness may mean sometimes saying "no") in your work environment. Forgive and let go. Engage in your career as a service to others. This is a beautiful space to be in. In the end, the Universe will love, be kind, forgive and be of service to you.

*My **purpose** is…*

This is the number one factor in blooming mentally, spiritually, physically and successfully in your career. Knowing your purpose brings greater fulfillment than money ever will in your career. Don't get me wrong, you should definitely get paid what you're worth, it's just that knowing your purpose will make your worth clearer to you and those around you. Knowing your purpose will help you leave the project or work site filling more complete by day's end.

Do you know your purpose? If so, great for you! Live in it! If you don't, make a commitment to find out what your purpose is before moving too far.

*God says **it's mine***.

Imagine that you were given a God-awesome, beautifully wrapped package. It's yours. You can unwrap it to discover its treasures, or you can ignore the box, never to see all the beauty it holds or the amazing experiences it will bring. You see it? That. Is. Yours. Own what you have been given. It's yours. Not mine. Not his. Not hers. Not anybody else's. It's yours. Now own it. Carry it and make your career more positively astounding than you've ever imagined. We're waiting.

Invest in YOU. Now.

You've been told this before, but you've been hesitant to do it. Try doing this NOW. Invest in You. That means allowing yourself time to rest. That means saying NO to things you clearly aren't admonished to do. That means spending money on your survival, including health, wealth, spirit and pure happiness. What about everybody else? Well, they can't get the best from you if you aren't investing to produce your best self.

Always invest in yourself.

When you invest in yourself, it shows others you value your blessing and sets a positive example for them. Yesterday, you did something great for yourself. Don't make this a once a year thing. <u>Always</u> invest in yourself. In big and small ways invest in a growing you.

For example, get enough sleep for your mind and body. Take that educational course you find interesting. If your body type will benefit from running regularly, run. If your body will benefit from tai chi, do it. If your body will benefit from walnuts, snack on a few today. Investing in you means a lot to you and those you influence.

No matter your stage in life, **keep growing**

Accept the fact that you can never professionally grow too much. Ever. The world is huge. Keep growing and keep sharing. Don't know how else to grow? Look up Amazon's bestselling books in the category you like. Try new restaurants, activities, and learning opportunities. Sign up for that conference you've always wanted to attend. Network and ask your friends what they've been up to and ask if they think you'll enjoy it too. Keep growing and enjoy every moment of it.

*Reach out for **help** today.*

No matter how "high" or "tall" you believe they are, reach out to individuals you find successful for insight. Reach out to that coworker. Send the executive leader you admire and ask her to mentor you. Though you may be scared or nervous, go for it anyway. Say something authentically generous and ask for a tip or two that relates to their own success.

Read. Listen. Watch. **Learn**.

Read, listen, watch, and learn what success looks like every day, so much so, that it becomes a habit. You will continuously gain something to promote a better you. You never know when you might find that piece of information that can start a professional conversation or a nugget that will change your career path.

Celebrate YOU

Celebrate every bit of your success, large or small! Often times, we just check an accomplishment off a list and keep moving. Why not celebrate? Celebrate YOU! Whether you do it in a big way or a small way, actually take the time to acknowledge the moment and celebrate what you've checked off the list. After this book is finished, I'm having a taste of one of my favorite deserts, flan. When the book hits the market, I'm having a party with my friends. What about you? What will you check off your list and how will you celebrate your accomplishment?

*You did good! Now **show 'em excellence**!*

"Good" was enough when you started. Once you're in the swing of things in your new role, embrace and display your excellence. Always aim to show a <u>great</u> representation of yourself. Believe it or not, sometimes it's a new outfit that makes you look and feel fierce. On the other hand, it may be digging deep into your idea to make business processes more efficient without hurting the bottom line.

*It's a **new** year!*

Can you tell I love this "It's a new year!" thingy no matter what day it is in the year? For those of you who believe it should be January before you continue, stop here and skip over this part, and go to the next bit of encouragement. For those of you who want to get your groove back now, keep going.

Remember all the excitement that takes place when the official New Year arrives? Let's grab that excitement again. The New Year is "here" so put your career ambitions back into gear.

Believe it or not,

you have what you need

You say you didn't go for it because you doubted you had enough to apply for the job. You didn't take the risk, because you feared you didn't have the education to qualify. My response is this, you have what you need to go for it. What do you have to lose when you apply for that coveted position? What would be traumatic about taking the educational course to succeed? If its money, ask your employer for support and see what happens. Go for it! You have what you need to move forward.

I didn't always get the role I wanted in my career.

Crew, it's true, we don't always get the role we had our eye on. That closed door could lead you to an open door to something much better. Know that most times, when you don't get the initial role you worked for, there is a surprise right around the corner. Most professionals will tell you that what they ended up grabbing was something they didn't consider before *or* that what they have now is much better. Don't stay down too long worrying about a role you didn't get, the better is on its way.

*Do "it" **differently** today.*

You've heard and have been told over and over again, "Do it." I challenge you to not only "do it," but do it **differently**. If you're a business owner, do something great, but differently this time for your customers, which your competitors are *not* doing. Speak up in business strategy meetings and propose something professionally that will help your team be more effective and innovative.

Think **like your competition** *thinks.*

This could be super fun! Think like your competitor thinks. Knowing how your competitors think is not just for sports athletes or someone looking for a date. It's also about career moves so that you can do things differently, better and positively unexpected. Once you understand the plays your competitors have, the better you're prepared to navigate the course to win with integrity in your career.

Tell them!

Often, the impedance to a successful interview is failing to tell the interviewer about your valuable skills and career wins. Know there are productive ways to sell yourself without sounding arrogant or feeling guilty. Check out my online videos about selling yourself. Let the interviewer clearly know just how VALUABLE you are. By sharing your skills and career wins, you'll be doing yourself *and* the interviewer a favor.

*Make the **story** relatable*

Practice telling your story in succinct, specific ways your listener can relate. Researchers and authors say that clear, succinct and relatable communication will make a huge impact to the person you're attempting to connect with. For example, don't just tell a manager who likes things done efficiently that you've completed the calculations and entered the data. Instead state you've *accurately* calculated the data *using newly incorporated quality controls* and entered the data all *while meeting the goal of completing the task sooner than the group has before.*

> *"Know that you have a purpose, a reason for existence, and **that reason is important**."*
>
> Excerpt from *RUSH: Embracing your purpose and all of the psychological thrillers it brings with it.* - Hope LeNoir

I'm huge on discovering and operating in your God-given purpose for your benefit and for the benefit for others. Your purpose is important for so many positively, fantastic reasons! Take at least half an hour today to learn more about your purpose and how you can use it.

*"Find that moment in your week or your day to sit and listen, receive and **rejuvenate your soul**."*

So many things to do. So many instructions to follow. Pause. Take a moment for yourself. AND don't feel guilty about it. You, taking a moment to rejuvenate and discover more about your soul has the potential to meaningfully touch so many people. Don't pass up that opportunity. Find that moment.

*"LESSON 1: **Be in every moment** of your life." - Hope LeNoir*

This is one of my favorite quotes from my book *RUSH*, because it reminds me of one of my biggest epiphanies. When you exist and observe yourself in this place called life, you discover so much about your purposed career path and the dynamics of others. This is when you appreciate your professional purpose and are more driven to grow it. It is in those moments that you gain higher perspective and greater goals. Be in those moments and enjoy it!

Know who ***you*** are and grow

One of the first pieces of advice I give to clients who don't know what career they want to be in is, "Know who you are." Knowing who you are makes directing your career ambitions clearer.

Be *visible*

One of the most influential things I've learned in my own career journey is to be visible. Consistently acting in silence doesn't get you where you want or need to be. Being visible helps others identify your value and where your skills can be better used. This doesn't mean overpowering others. It means making your achievements and potential apparent so that you can be in the right place to help move the team toward the overall goal.

*Network and **network** some more*

I use this word, network, hesitantly. This doesn't mean checking off how many times you've presented an elevator pitch. To me, networking is more about meeting new professionals and building professional relationships with them. This is a way to genuinely get to know people, who they are, what connections they have, and what insight they can offer you and your goals. This is also a way for you to know where to use your skills to help them.

Discover *the depths of your purpose.*

If you've actually been acting on the tips given to you, you would have begun identifying your true career purpose by now. ☺ Whooo hoooo! You go! Keep digging into your purpose today. What does it mean and how does it feel to you? Share with us!

*What's the **BEST thing** your boss gave you?*

Loaded question, huh? Really. Think about it. What is one of the greatest things one of your leaders have given you? If you know how to contact that person, send them a card, email or stop by their desk to remind them about the gift, how much it meant to you and how you were able to use it in your career growth. It means a lot for a leader to know how they've helped someone else in a positive way. I hope you get the same positive experience many times in the future.

Create and recite ***your own mantra***

Obviously one of my mantra's is "I will Rise and Fly." You should have one too. This will remind you how strong and capable you are. It's also a way of motivating you to move forward. To that end, if you said it, why not commit yourself to seeing it through? What if I've already risen and flown? Glad you asked. ☺ Well, that just means I need to rise higher and fly further and bring other professionals along the way.

*Have a **funny tidbit**.*

I am the worst comedian ever. Ever. BUT I try. Maybe you're already an expert at telling a decent joke or have a funny story in your pocket. Great! Be open to sharing it (when appropriate of course). This way you have a funny story ready to share and put smiles on your peers' faces during the day. Disclaimer: Don't overdo it!

*Tell what I **see in flight**.*

Whenever you see market opportunities, share with your leader. Also share how your business can be a part of that flight. Your insight is needed. The more you do this, the more helpful you can become and the more drive you'll have to learn and grow.

*You have to **be a part** of nonlinear innovation.*

Work and career pathing are not the same as it was years ago. The workforce as it is today and how it will be in the future is faster and more innovative. The way to excel is not to move in a straight line in an effort to innovate, it's moving in a nonlinear journey. That means thinking like an outsider. Sometimes forward, but sometimes backward. Sometimes intricately. Most times simply.

Brand it

Today is a critical moment to make your brand solid. Thinking about what you do now affects your brand in the future. First, recall who you said you are. Now restate your purpose. Next step is to be consistent about the behaviors, including what you say. Confirm who you said you are and what your purpose is in your life and career. That's your brand. Keep that solid.

Use *your **imagination*** *to create AND enhance.*

Remember that super creative stuff you used to do and think about decades ago? Bring it back! Tap into that imagination of yours and bring out crazy creations like never before that will enhance the business around you. Start by identifying the gaps and thinking of ways to close them.

Unwrap your gift.

For so long, I've seen so many people who clearly know their gift but refuse to actually show and use their gift. Often times we're scared. Sometimes we underappreciate what we have to give. Don't let that happen for you. Unwrap your gift. Show those around you. Use it to help build fulfillment and greatness within you and around you!

You belong here.

Sometimes it takes a friend or colleague to remind you not to doubt your success and why you're in a particular role. I had a colleague to do that for me. I am so grateful for that, so I pass that important confirmation on to you. It is true. Everyone is in a particular place for a reason. We each have a purpose in the space we're in. When I say each, that means you too! KNOW THAT YOU BELONG HERE!

Now that you know this for sure, think about why you belong and what you are designed to bring. Now, bring it because you belong in this space.

Start your own "**new normal**."

Forget about what's normal. Do you. Create and embrace the positive normal for you. It's yours. Now, release your new normal and feel comfortable about it. Experience the possibilities your new normal will bring to your career and others.

Own the moment, *whether good or bad.*

It happened, so go ahead and own it. This DOES NOT mean that any of it was your fault, but the response is in your hands. What has happened in your career could teach you something, expose your greatness, or even place you in a new role. Yep. I went there. Own it. Think about what has happened and how you can use it to your advantage with integrity.

Give great energy.

Did you know that your energy influences the behavior and energy of those around you? Think about how you feel if negative people surround you. Think about how that would make you behave and what it will make you want to say. Be one of the people who exudes great energy before you leave your home and when you arrive at work. Imagine how this will have a great impact on your day, your perception of self and others, and your influence!

Identify *the problem then **offer** the solution.*

If you've identified a problem in your work environment, bring it to up to the right people who could help you make positive changes. Offer solutions to that problem. This technique will improve the organization, make you stand out, and grow your team. Stop accepting problems, and start voicing and supporting great solutions.

EQ skills **enhance the experience**
for you and them.

Have you examined your emotional intelligence? Now is the time. Studies show that higher EQ is a greater indicator of success than high IQ in individuals. The great news is you can improve your EQ. Even if you've taken the EQ test before, you can work to improve and then take the test again. You will find great resources about emotional intelligence online. Try them. This will help you better engage in your work environment with colleagues.

Iteration

Iteration means to repeat a process until you reach the desired result. Deliver your goodness in the workforce and set the expectation that your next step is to deliver even better with the next version. Consider not waiting and waiting and waiting and waiting and waiting (I think you get it) to deliver until you think everything is perfect.

Prodigy

Years ago, I began to be labeled the "Professional Prodigy." A prodigy is something extraordinary. **You** too are extraordinary so show it! What is that great thing that you do? Build it into your brand today. Whatever that thing is, declare that's who you are and what you represent all day. Use the following days to build that thing into what you are known for. Since I'm the professional prodigy, which prodigy are you??

*Create your own **role**!*

Don't know what you want to do in your career? Or, do you know what you want to do, but can't find a job that fits? Then create your own role. I once worked for a corporation that didn't have the role I wanted. I went to my leader and made it clear exactly what I wanted to do and how I could make it happen without monetary or time costs to him. He said, "Go for it!" I did it and it became one of the most popular activities in the region. In addition, I had the opportunity to grow and exhibit my purpose, touch many lives, and have lots of fun! If you don't see the role you like where you are, but don't want to switch companies, create your own role or duties as an in-house side gig!

Know who *you are.*

Explore who you are this weekend. Make time and expand what you learned about yourself. For example, I learned I am a leader. I expanded on what I learned and discovered I am a servant leader. (There's a book about that.) Knowing who you are and the strengths you have will help you grow your skills and help you answer big questions in an interview.

Take the weekend to find out some cool discoveries about you. Tap into your strengths *and* identify your weaknesses. There is soooo much more to learn about you and your professional style.

When I grow up, I want to be

just like me.

Are you able to honestly say this? "When I grow up, I want to be just like me." Imagine the future you. The best you. The you that you want to be. What does that look like? What is the greatness you bring to the world? Who are you surrounded by? Turn the wonderful future you in your imagination into a reality today! What you'll discover is you're more than you ever imagined. That person is the person who you want to be like.

*Yes, **perception** is important.*

According to Webster's dictionary, perception is a mental image. Research will tell you that perception, whether we want it to be or not, is important. You have the ability to own how most people perceive you. Though not everyone will "get you" (or like you, and that's okay), make sure your perception is as clear and consistent as possible. You are the "go to" person for what? What can you be trusted with? What do you stand for? What will be your likely response to a tough professional situation? Create a solid, positive, influential and consistent perception of yourself.

Set a *descriptive goal*.

Yes. I'm telling you to imagine your goal to the fullest. Don't settle for, "I'm going to get an increase in salary." Don't aim for "I'm going to meet more people this year." Go all out and be more descriptive with your goal. An example of a more descriptive goal is "I'm going to meet one new person a week in my business field this year." Another example is "On Tuesday, I'm going to take the steps my coach has given me to improve my salary." Be intentional and specific. Oh, and don't forget to write it down. (Smile)

*You are **ah- mazing**!*

I'm not sure you're giving yourself enough credit for all that you've done. It's been a long time and a lot of hard work. You may think what you've accomplished thus far is small, but it is HUGE. Great job. Keep going, and be sure to *celebrate your wins*. Last but not least, keep being amazing.

Keep asking questions

Keep asking questions, even if you think you know what you're doing. Avoid attempting to solve what most people see on the surface, go for the root or the REAL business issues and challenges. Though you may offer solutions along the way, there's nothing like getting to the core of the problem and offering a *resolution*. That's what's going to get you ahead.

Promote *– to contribute to the growth or prosperity of (...from Webster's dictionary)*

I know you have a divine purpose. I know you have a fantastic skill ready for a growth spurt. Because of this, I promote you. You deserve it! The question is, do YOU believe in you? Then promote yourself. Go to any of my social media sites and promote yourself - TODAY. Tell the world what great skill you have and that you're working to make it even more phenomenal. The platform is open to you. Bring that excitement that all of us are waiting for! Take the time to tell us about your success on Facebook! Others who've read up to this point are sharing their success too!

www.facebook.com/RiseandFly

*Have you **repeat**ed your quote?*

First step was to define who you are. Don't make a long job out of it. Off the bat, who are you? Who do you want to become? If you haven't already, write it down (seeing a trend?), and put it where you can view it every morning. As you start your day, repeat your quote. It's yours. Claim it.

*Let them **watch**.*

Studies tell us that people are always watching whether we know it or not. Allow us to watch your greatness. Give us something EXCEPTIONAL to look at. Give us something different to talk about. Be the example. Be the difference at work. Be that go-to person for the thing you are purposed to do. Let them watch. I dare you.

*The **writing is on the wall**, so make what you see yours.*

Ever noticed the role you've been craving is always in your face? Ever noticed that when there's an opening you're interested in, you never feel quite ready? Noticed that same position is on your Vision Board? The writing in on the wall. Every. Where. Grab the confidence, skill and network to make it yours. Go for it. You've got this!

*What's **next**?*

Okay, now you're thinking about retiring or you and your employer are "breaking up." What now? What's next? I'm glad you asked. Go back to being solid about what you're *purposed* to do professionally. How can your Higher Power help you do that? Well, that's what's next.

*There's **good** and there's **great**.*

Get out of the mindset of "I'm doing what my job description says I should do, isn't that enough?" That state of mind is long gone in the workplace. The world is excited about seeing more of your creativity. Don't be good according to the description of your job role. Go further. Be GREAT while visibly and positively impacting yourself and others. That's what helps catapult careers!

Don't *let the work consume you.*

This book is full of pushes and encouragement to identify, build, and grow the very best YOU. What I wouldn't push for or encourage is to let your job consume you. Stick with what you're destined to do. Let go of what others mistakenly THINK you should do or what is seen as the TRADITIONAL work when you know something else, or rest, is better for you. Don't do work just because. "Just because" is NOT good for your spirit, your health, your happiness, or the people you intend to touch.

Thankful *for the mornings*

Every morning, take a moment to see the beauty in front of you. What is it that you are grateful for? Acknowledge that thing, whether it's the sound of your favorite song on your alarm or the promotion you got yesterday. Maybe it's being able to go for a stroll at lunch. Possibly it's finally being able to take a true, relaxing vacation. Maybe it's waking up and finally feeling the confidence and support you need for that next job. See the wonderful things every morning, and don't forget to say, "thank you."

Recovery is something you can do

Though you bend, don't break. You have what it takes to straighten up and get back in it. Every professional has or will be broken in their career, but each one of us have what it takes to recover from whatever it was that brought us down. *Resilience* is key. You can recover.

Be true *to your purpose.*

I can't stress this enough. Be true to your purpose. There are countless benefits true purpose will bring to your career, like the idea of realized fulfillment in your professional endeavors. In addition, operating purposefully will give you more drive in your career as well as develop your professional voice and brand.

Know who you are and grow!

In coaching sessions, when clients ask how to identify their next career move, I start with the statement, "Know who you are." This is the first key step. Having a solid idea of who you are helps you target the roles you want to be in as well as build a clear and noticeable brand. Know yourself. Start by reading insightful books like *Strengths Finder* by Tom Rath and living in every professional moment like my book *RUSH* suggests. Dig deep. You'll have fun here and be amazed by all that you will find!

*Connect with someone **better than you***

Find professionals who are extremely phenomenal in their career. The type of career you are pursuing that is. Connect with that person to learn how they got there. Take in the amazing (and sometimes heartfelt) insights they give you and tailor it to what you need to be even more successful. I did and unearthed professional tips that I might not have thought of on my own, which in the end, made me one of those phenomenal individuals who others reach out to.

New and blunt ***interview techniques HERE***.

Think like your best competition thinks. Let the interviewer clearly know just how VALUABLE you are. Make it easy for them to make the hiring decision. It's not about bragging or being boastful—it's about making it worth your and the interviewer's time. It's about giving the information he or she is hoping to hear. Give them relatable and smart details about how you've used your skills, talents, and gifts to get needed results. As an interviewer myself, this always makes the decision process a no-brainer for me.

*Challenging times are **opportunistic times**.*

It may not be what you want to hear or read. Yes, I know you've heard it before. Challenging times are the opportunistic times. Wait, hear me out. Challenging times are the right times to take advantage of the opportunity the challenge presents to you. Identify the core of the challenge and get with the right people to help you understand what it takes to move forward. Through it all, you'll learn so much about yourself and ways to close the business gap.

*Do it **differently** today.*

Think about how things can be done differently and better. Everyday everybody wants things to be better. Look for the professional gaps today and find ways to use your skills to improve them. Keep it simple, just think "I will make things better." Be among those who make a big difference through the small changes that you were able to identify.

Employee Resource Groups rock!

Does your company have an Employee Resource Group? If you don't know, find out. If they do, investigate them and what they represent. You can meet a lot of influential professionals in your company's Employee Resource Groups. Some may be very tenure and some new to the company, which means there are a variety of resources to get a lot of information about the company and career pathing. You may also find out some of the ERG events can be a lot of fun and offer cultural awareness you're looking for at work.

If your company does not have an ERG, find out ways to start one!

Open the feedback box

If you don't consider your feedback as a gift, think of it as the "present." Either way, feedback can be beneficial to you and the situation. Open the feedback gift given to you and be open to what it is that you see. Discover how it will help you or if it is something you should just toss. (But don't toss it too fast.) Ask yourself, what can I gain from this feedback? How can I be a better professional based on this feedback? How will this feedback help me strengthen the brand I want for myself?

*Invest in **YOU**.*

Take the time to make investments in your career growth, whether you're an associate, people leader or solo entrepreneur. Today, search for and schedule sessions, conferences and events that will help you build your skill and your clientele. Some will be free. Some might be costly. Start by listing them with the date and the price. Then scrutinize them and choose the best ones for you. You'll thank me for it.

Monday is not Friday, *but you knew that, right?*

If your Monday was not what you wanted it to be, there is still time. Your Monday will not be like your Friday. Take the opportunity to make the difference happen. THAT happened, now is the time to resolve the issue. Engage in the excitement and make the next day better. Then make the next day even better. Look at it this way, Monday is NOT Friday and though Monday was not your favorite, there's still an opportunity to make Monday epic.

Pssssst, **SELL** *YOURSELF!*

One of my favorite events was my *Sell Yourself* event! It was inspiring to watch attendees feel absolutely empowered to tell the world all about their professional skills and career endeavors. Don't feel afraid to tell people how skilled you are and what you've accomplished. Don't be hesitant either. There is a way to share your greatness without feeling arrogant. Actually, *Sell Yourself* was designed to show people how liberating, healthy and important it is for each of us to tell people about your skills.

*What **inspires** you?*

One of the most motivating ways to stay on or get back on track and move forward with your career goals is to easily identify what inspires you in a positive way. What is it that makes you smile? What is it that gets you excited about working toward the goal until the end? Ponder that today and use that to get you back on the road.

What do you **want them to say***?*
Portray the description.

What is it you want people to say about you? Portray that description. For example, do you want people to say how honest you are? Be honest, the right way, about how you believe the business can improve. Want people to say you have good ideas? Be vocal about your ideas and outline the research you've done on ways your ideas can benefit the team. Be the description you want others to use. Need help? Get ideas from a trusted friend, coach or mentor on how you can authentically be that person.

*Know who you are and **boldly execute**
on your strengths.*

One of the greatest things I've done in my career is to KNOW, I mean really KNOW my strengths. I realized this is the greatest way I could give back to the people I and my business serve. Not only was this a great way to identify how to best build my career and serve others, but it was also a great way to build a solid brand! One of the books that I've read to help get me there is *Strengths Finder 2.0.* by Tom Rath. If you haven't already, consider using this book as a great tool for you as well.

*No here, but **yes there**.*

At some point, you have to intentionally determine when to say "no" here, but "yes" there. You know this, right? Well it's true. You shouldn't say "Yes" to everything thrown your way. If you do, you'll be depleted by everything given to you. Today, focus on what is best for you and the career goals you're trying to meet. When you say "no," follow up with a suggestion to still get the job done.

Come on. **You did it**!

Your accomplishments aren't small. Know the things you do, which you think are small, are actually HUGE and AMAZING. Keep impacting lives with your professional skill and really feel good about it along the way!

You belong here.

Ever been in a dream role, but start to believe you don't belong there? Stop. You are there for a reason, and most importantly, you belong there. Know that you deserve to be in that great place and there is even more for you after that. Accept the greatness. Celebrate it! Grow it! Show appreciation for it! It belongs to you!

Include a ***fantastic mentor***.

The most incredible professionals have or had a great mentor. A mentor is someone you trust, who's had experiences you can learn from, who can give you good guidance and support. They are invested in you and have your best interest at heart. You don't have to figure out everything slowly on your own. You can grow and celebrate your success with others. In other words, like other incredibly successful professionals, you shouldn't be alone in your career journey either. Look for and stay connected to a great mentor.

*When the industry **shifts**, make an update.*

One of the worst things you can do in your career is to remain stagnant in your career thoughts, processes, and behaviors when your industry changes. Consider understanding *how* the industry is changing and how you can contribute to those changes. Research where your industry is heading in the future so you can prepare the way for yourself and the organization. If you've been one of my followers, you've consistently been updating your professional strengths, so they are ready to be used. Fret not about professional shifts! This could be fun and super rewarding!

*What have you **volunteer**ed for lately?*

Part of having a successful life and career is taking the time to volunteer to help others. As others have helped you along the way, you can pay it forward and help those who need your help. This can be super fulfilling. Choose your favorite nonprofit organization that will allow you to use your strengths, but don't unnecessarily take up all of your time.

Use your voice *to make things right.*

If you sense something went wrong in your business group, use your voice to help make it right. Overlooking the issue is not the answer. I learned this lesson a long time ago when I attempted to overlook an issue at work. A leader reminded me I should consider professionals who would take the place after me. Addressing the elephant in the room, the right way, whether it's one on one or even with an HR professional, will help all those involved.

Community connections are *valuable.*

Connect with respectable new and current friends in your community. It's a good way to grab a professional tip or two that you wouldn't get on the job. Make sure these connections are a group of individuals who have a totally different perspective than colleagues at work. They also have different *experiences* than your colleagues. Your community connections will trigger creative ideas you can develop and use in your career.

IMAGINE BEFORE.

Before you even see it manifest, I dare you to imagine your life the exact way you want it to be. Imagine your everyday career activities. Imagine what your title will be. Imagine the emotions of the clients you serve. Imagine what they look like and what they will say to you. Imagine how you will feel once you've noticed what you've imagined is reality. Now connect a plan with that dream in mind.

Talent = Opportunity.

If you're reading this, you have a talent! If you have a talent, you have an opportunity. If you haven't already figured out what that talent is, now is the time! Here's a chance to see how your talent can be grown and how it can work for you!

With your criticism, **bring a solution**.

It's great to critique a career situation or professional process. However, never leave without suggesting a solution to what you've observed. Be a problem solver, not a complainer. Your ideas are what will help drive your success and business success forward.

Always be a point ahead.

Make every day of your career a day that you are ahead of the game. This way you're always ready for the next big move, not fiercely *trying* to get ready for the next big move.

*Build*ing a Friday **Adventure**

This is one of my favorite Facebook posts! "Just because it's Friday doesn't mean you have to wait until Monday. If the excitement hits, draft ways to make Monday a positive career move." Have your Mondays set a positive tone for your week, quarter, year, and life!

Move with **intention**

Your career moves should have the best intentions. With every decision you make, you definitely intend to make the right moves with intention and integrity. It may not turn out to be what you want or what you thought was best, be you'll feel good knowing what you did had the best intentions at heart. It also reinforces your brand with integrity.

IMAGINE AFTER

You've found your purpose. You've come up with a plan to reach your first set of goals. You're building your professional purpose with excitement. You've imagined what success will look like for you. You are on your way there. Now, imagine how you'll celebrate your success after you've reached your goal. What will you do? How will you celebrate? How will you give thanks for all that you've been given to accomplish your goal? Imagine the after and really be prepared for the gratuitous celebration you've imagined!

*You have **great ideas***

Through all of your career efforts, remain authentic in your ideas, true to your values, and faithful to the right goals. You have great ideas. Be the best you can be by sharing those ideas. People will appreciate your transparency and integrity when you share. Not to mention, you will feel great showing *you*.

Get uncomfortable. **Stretch.**

Just like physically stretching is a good way to stay physically flexible, professionally stretching is a good way to stay professionally flexible. Once you've reached one goal, consider ways to continue to grow your skill and experience. Don't be afraid of being in a little discomfort, as long as it's a healthy and a respectable choice. Stretch yourself in your career and watch yourself reach new heights.

*Go the extra mile-**that way**.*

Part of being successful in your career is going the extra mile. But wait. This doesn't mean doing a lot of stuff or always working extra-long hours. It means engaging in the right behaviors and going the extra mile as aligned with your professional skill. It means doing a little more to get to your dream career. The goal here is not to simply do a lot of stuff, but to do the *right* stuff in excellence that reflect the brand you want visible to decision-makers.

*Work hard, **rest** well.*

Working hard in your career can be appreciated. Resting well can also be appreciated. More importantly, resting is also *necessary*. We've all heard stories of sleep deprived go-getters, going above and beyond and doing things others refuse to do as the way to get ahead. What people often fail to tell is the essentialness of resting as a part of the journey to the top. Make sure you get the rest you need. Get the amount of sleep you need. Stop moving when your body of instincts tell you to stop. Recharge and feel good about what you've already done. Work hard. Rest well.

Take charge *of your career.*

Meeting your career goals involves a lot of stakeholders and supporters, however, you must personally own your career journey. Ownership means following through with fresh development courses and experiences. It means staying connected to great influencers. It means accepting accountability for mistakes or misgivings. And of course, I have to mention it, celebrating what you've already accomplished!

Identify your career style.

Is your style identifying gaps or executing on expectations? Is your career style to move forward proactively or when you've been told to move? Is your style to be clear about your capabilities or assume that everyone will definitely take notice? Take today to really dig deep to determine your career style. Write it down. Take a look at it. If you're driving right now, simply think about examples where you have exhibited these types of styles. Now evaluate whether or not this is the right style to pursue your career goals or should you attempt to redirect how you engage in your career.

*It's all **about you.***

I once told one of my bosses that I didn't want to accept a new role because I wanted to be there for my growing team. He reminded me that I am a priority for the decisions I make. This may make you feel uncomfortable, however, it had to be said to me and it should be said to you. You are a priority. Prioritize yourself within your own career journey. Do what's important for you. You will find it is indeed necessary for all those around you.

*You have what it takes to **sparkle** from a setback.*

There are certainly career misadventures that really hurt. There are career setbacks that really make you angry. Despite who or what was wrong in this situation, learn from that situation and make your next career move a phenomenal comeback!

Professionally **connect with movers.**

Career-movers that is. Right now, build professional relationships with professionals who are succeeding in their career. It's great to connect with peers and friendly people, however, know that it is also great to connect with professionals who have been where you are and can offer particular insight based on relative experiences.

*The gift is in the **details**.*

Get rid of, "What feedback do you have for me?" Be more specific about the feedback you need. The more you're specific, there more you'll receive. For example, do you need feedback on a speech you just gave? Do you need feedback on your effectiveness with delegating? From this day forward, engage the leader(s) you trust for specific feedback.

~~*Why you think you can't.*~~ *Why you think* ***you will***.

Stop spending time on WHY you think you can't! Take all of those negative feelings out of your life and spend time on why you think you can. As a matter of fact, believe that you can—and will! You'll get a lot further believing that you can. <u>How</u> you can will then become a lot clearer.

Don't take *failure for granted.*

This is a hard pill to swallow. Remember it is this scary pill that could make you a lot healthier professionally. The first step is analyzing what happened. What could you have done differently? What factors influenced the failure? How can you grow from this failure?

Allow the discoveries associated with failure to help you, not halt you. Failure is an unasked for gift that leads us towards a better route in our journey. Don't take it for granted.

Influence the world through your career.

Did you know you can influence the world through your career? Do you know how influential your contributions are to the clients who use your product or service? Your contribution is then a chain reaction to the rest of the world. Be proud of your contributions and its impact to the big picture.

Keep those ***ideas in a great place.***

You always have good ideas. Just so you don't forget, jot down those ideas as they come to you. Use those left-over notebooks or neat notebooks you got for free at the last event you attended. Keep a notebook in your purse or backpack with an extra pen. Keep a notebook in your car. Better yet, keep notes on the thing you always carry with you, like your mobile device. You never know when an opportunity to present your great ideas will come. You'll thank me for this "write down your ideas" tip later.

Appreciate your accomplishments.

You did that! You've accomplished so much lately. Appreciate it. Document it. I've documented every success I've know I've had. It has been a wonderful resource for new ideas! It is also a reminder of how much I accomplished and confirmation of what I am capable of doing. Scrolling through your accomplishments can bring the same sort of ammo for you too!

Your health is more important
than your career.

I believe in working hard. I believe in going above and beyond. I don't believe in your career taking YOU. Don't allow your career to damage your physical health. If you recognize your career is damaging your physical health, step back and look for ways to make things better. Try going for walks, shifting your role, or taking advantage of the complimentary health benefits at work. Whatever happens, please, always take of you.

*It's **not just for church**.*

Remember, your purpose is not just for church events. The purpose given to you should be used in even more endeavors. What you will find is that knowing and *applying* your purpose to the work you do every day will enhance your life. Just a little truth nugget: When your purpose connects with your career, your career becomes more meaningful.

*Make better **even better**.*

Take a look at the best and feel the excitement of making it even better. Never settle for good enough. What are some of the best parts of your career? What are some of the best parts about your business? Now that you know this, how can you make it better? Make things faster. Clearer. More exciting. Simply better. I can't wait to hear what you've done!

Acknowledge the problem and **offer a solution.**

It's important to make others aware of problems in the work environment. It is also important to offer a solution to that problem. To that end, whenever you give facts about a problem, offer a solution. This way, it's more likely you'll be heard.

Tell the right people about your idea!

Let go of angst and fear. Talk to encouragers. Read inspiring pieces. Watch videos that prepare you. Find out who are the right people at your job to pitch your idea. Don't forget to find out more about the personalities of the right people. Go ahead and propose that great idea you've been holding on to!

Extraordinary behavior =
extraordinary brand.

Clearly define yourself in all that you say and do. Practice being the positive career accomplisher you say you want to become. Now that you know who you are and what you want your brand to be, make sure your behavior aligns with that extraordinary brand. You're so there.

Bring out ***your positive vibe***.

Invoke a positive feeling to make your work project memorable. Your light has the ability to change the perspective of your working environment. Your belief that things will go well can influence the behavior of others. In other words, your positive vibe has a lot of what you (and others) may need to move a project forward.

Remember your **career dreams**.

I know your career ambitions keep crossing your mind. Don't let it fall. Pick it back up! Stay committed to those career dreams you wanted to make a reality. Don't just let your dreams float around in your mind or be forgotten. Pick them up, dust them off and watch them work.

*Always **aim to be** a **better** you.*

I once worked for a group whose leaders were big on development. I admired that tremendously. I remember publicly posting my career story to let them know that continuously developing will always be a part of my career, even when I turn 97. No matter your age or your position, always aim to be better for yourself and for others!

Make today **a great day**.

I'm used to hearing, "Have a good day." It wasn't until someone once told me to "make it a great day" that I realized I just might have the power to make this day a great one! I don't have to merely *accept* the day I am given. I can influence the day I desire. You have the power to make this day a great one too. What will you do today not just to *have*, but to **make** it a great day?

*Have you **searched online** for it yet?*

In this day and age most searches for the next great thing are done online. Today, search online to find the next great career opportunity, book, coach or professional development course. See what people are saying about how to build and display the value you bring to the table.

Challenges are a *beautiful opportunity*.

Challenges set the stage for something greater than you can imagine. Challenges allow you to stretch yourself beyond what you thought you could. They also provide avenues for you to accomplish career goals like never before. Be receptive to a good challenge and watch your career go to an amazing place.

Tell them about **your strengths**.

Does everyone around you know your strengths? Don't just make your strengths visible, make your strengths heard. Make it easy for others to see and memorable for them to reference. Let them know what you'd be a great resource for and why they can trust you'd be a perfect option for a future opening in that area.

Focus *on what you aim to be.*

Doing too much of varied tasks can lead to the perception you are a person that people can delegate a lot of work. Instead, get involved in a lot of what you <u>want</u> to be involved. Be intentional about doing the work relative to your career goals. Put your focus on the opportunities that help you reach where you aim to be.

Do one thing.

What is one small thing you can do *today* to get you closer to your dream? Pick something quick that aligns with your career goals. Let me help you out here. Perhaps you can send a quick email to a professional you'd love to connect with. Maybe it's making a list of some of the professional goals you want to accomplish over the next three months. Whatever it is, list it. Now take an hour today to do one of those things that prepares you for your career dream. Pssst—Do all of this again tomorrow.

*Remind yourself that **you are** **AMAZING**.*

I've said it several times, either in this book or on my social site – You are amazing! Sometimes you have to remind yourself of this too. You are indeed amazing and you have amazing capabilities. Go into new career adventures with confidence. Know that if you love a role that's in your life's purpose, you can either do it now OR that you will figure it out. Why do I say that? Because you are amazing, and I believe in you!

Don't just rise. ***Fly*** *too.*

I love the idea of "rising and flying." It is a reminder not to just rise up from the ashes but take off and fly! How empowering and exciting is that? Whatever has happened in your career, good or bad, rise up above it. Then take off to higher heights!

Listen to and ***watch*** successful people.

Don't try to grab your goal on your own. Why would you have to do that? Take the opportunity to observe and learn from people who've already gained the success you're hoping to reach. Take note of some of the things they talk about. Discover their habits that help them succeed. Check out what matters most to them and how they communicate with others. You'll find that some of the things you observe, you don't want to do. You'll also find that some of the things you observe are duplicable and can be tailored to advance your career goals.

*Don't keep your smarts **wrapped up**.*

You are smart and this can be sooooooooo approachable. Don't keep that under wraps. Your industry needs what you have to make businesses and processes better, so show them your smarts. Scared? Practice with friends today. Use friends who you trust to give you good feedback about your approach. Feeling brave, and want to try with a group you don't know first? Go for it. Feel free to tell us about your smarts on my social media pages. We'd love to hear all about it!

*Choose to **step forward**.*

Get out of the monotony. Stop trying to do the same ol' thing in an effort to just get the work done. Omit the idea that you're not ready or not good enough. Remember what I said before? You are amazing, so choose to step forward. Take the opportunity to do something differently today. Offer a resolution to your team on ways work can be done more efficiently or effectively. Go for the role that you've been watching and is finally open. Once you step forward, chose to embrace the experience and get ready to step forward again.

With goals come (simple) plans. **_With plans come actions_**.

Have you set your goal yet? Great! Now create a plan to achieve the goal. It doesn't have to be complex. Keep your plan simple, but clear and intentional. Your plan could even be a one-page checklist. This may make reaching your goal feel more attainable. Once you have the plan, take action to make your goal your reality.

*You should **ask for things to be different***

I once was checking out at a store when the clerk randomly said to me, "I wish they'd play different music." Of course, confusion showed all over my face. "I wish they'd play different music in this store. They always play this stuff people don't like."

"Oh," I responded as I gave him my cash. "Did you ask the manager to change the music?" He replied no and said he didn't think she would consider his recommendation. I explained he wouldn't know if he didn't ask, and told him about another guy at a café who asked for a music change and succeeded in obtaining a different genre of music to be played in the café once a week. Want things to be different? Ask for it and explain why it would be better. You just might be surprised by the response.

*Let's get this day **started right**.*

Hi there! I'm glad I'm one of the first things you read or listened to today. I'm with you on this day. Let's clutch positive vibes, giggles, and confidence. We're going to get this day started right! Make it one of your greatest days. Whatever positive career move you make today, do it extremely well. You ready? Let's go!

*Stare at your motivation. Now **move forward.***

For a few seconds, stare at your motivation. Is it the title of a song? Perhaps it's a person who drives you. It may be a picture of a place you want to be or new computer devices you'd love to own. Stare at that. If your motivation is a live person, don't stare at them, without them knowing what you're doing. That can be creepy! Consider something about them that motivates you, like the type of books they read. Yep, stare at that. Now that you've absorbed your motivation, take that energy and move forward.

Leave your mark *before the end of your workday Friday*

You may have to work Saturday, but I challenge you to leave a mark in your work environment before you leave Friday. Remind yourself of the brand you want to have and do something that reinforces that brand. Do you want to be known for finishing projects accurately? Double check your work before you leave. Do you want to be known as someone with great organizational skills? Layout your presentation or even your desk using those organizational skills. How about making your great accomplishments visible? Type a short summary of your accomplishments for the week and send it to your leader.

Say it with me. **"I am confident about being great."**

At first, we may have to simply say it for ourselves before we start believing it is true. That's why I encourage you to say this with me, "I am confident about being great." Don't add any extras with it. Just say that sentence. "I am confident about being great." Think it, say it, and avoid adding anything else to it, especially a "but." "I am confident about being great." Ah, there you go. You said it. Believe it, because you are great and you're not afraid of it.

Breathe *in those ideas and breathe out your greatness.*

There are always new, great ideas for you to harvest. Keep looking for and plucking them from your idea tree. Take only the great ones in, I mean. Use those great ones to continue to build on ways you can make your career experiences and business ideas even stronger. Don't only go to traditional business conferences to build your ideas. Consider events that you've never experienced before. For example, I went to a magic show for the deaf, had a blast, and got so many business ideas!

*Don't **mistake being busy** as a reason for being rewarded.*

Make sure the work you're putting in is productive and helps you achieve your career goals. In other words, don't stay busy to look busy or helpful. This technique often works against the most skilled professionals. It often only brings more busy work. Work with purpose. Take on tasks that build the brand you want to have as well as visibility for the skill you want others to see.

Make something fabulous happen today.

You can do this! You have control to do this. Don't wait for someone to make the day fabulous for you. Make something fabulous happen today yourself. Choose the fabulous thing you can do and do that. Prefer to give something instead of do something? Then strategically give that fabulous thing today.

Edit your career journey.

Had a plan, but see a new opportunity to meet your goals? Then you need to edit your journey. Know that editing your journey is okay. Successful professionals do it all the time. This doesn't mean your goal has changed. It just means due to construction or unforeseen events, the route to get there has changed. Maybe a shortcut presented itself! Edit your career journey to make your professional dreams a reality.

*You're **not too old**!*

Forget about your age and all the accomplishments you thought you should have made by this time in your life. Forget about whether or not you're getting hired due to your age. Think about the skills you actually have, the experience you bring that others cannot yet bring. That is your box of gold. If you're still alive, you still have a purpose you can use in a great career endeavor. Now, I ask you to accept that you're not too old.

Pursue confidence.

Confidence, when used the right way, has so many benefits. It's not just about how you appear to others—it's what you believe about yourself. It's also about achieving goals and changing perspectives. It informs others how to see you. It's about believing in yourself and all of the capabilities of your magnificent Higher Power. Pursue confidence. Believe in yourself, your career abilities, and all of the good that comes with it.

Create the career *you've dreamed about.*

Think about a way you can create the career you want all while keeping the career you already have. It doesn't have to be complex or tiring. Keep it simple. Ask your leader if she or he minds if you volunteer for a certain project that will help the team grow. For example, do you want to be a project manager? Ask your leader if you can take time to lead a project for your team. Want to be an expert in artificial intelligence? Learn more about AI and how it can help your team be more efficient. Think about what you want your career to be like, then create the opportunity if it doesn't already exist.

*It's a great day to **relax**.*

I see you! You've worked really hard to get where you are. That's great! Now you certainly need to take the time to relax. I mean really relax. Take an extra nap. Go for a walk. Cuddle up and watch your favorite show. Whatever your relaxing technique is, use it. Rejuvenate yourself for the next exciting round of happiness and accomplishments.

Excited yet?

It's true, the world is your canvas. Imagine and get excited about what you will bring to the world tomorrow. By now you've been examining your purpose in life and thus your purpose in your career. You have been reminded and can feel how great and valuable you are to the world around you. Get excited. The world is waiting for what you will bring.

Decide to **be super extraordinary**.

I'm sure you've heard that one of the first steps to success is making the decision to do something. I challenge you to decide to be super extraordinary. Decide that today you will start doing all the great things you learned. Decide you will demonstrate all of your great capabilities. Decide. Now do.

*Attitudes are **not anonymous**.*

Your attitude says a lot about your abilities and your professionalism. With everything you do, an attitude comes with it. Make sure that you have the right attitude. Want to know what the right attitude is? Observe the attitudes of the people around you. What are some of the attitudes that light you up? What are some of the attitudes that light others up? What are some of the attitudes that make things happen in your work environment? See how much of a difference a positive attitude makes.

Be deliberate *about the career moves you make.*

Make deliberate career moves that are the best for YOU. Be intentional about the roles you apply for. Ask yourself, is this role aligned with your purpose? Will this role help you learn new skills to gain the experience you need? Will this role give you positive exposure to influential people? Be deliberate about your decisions when making the next career move. You'll be happy you did.

*It's **not just about you***

Yes. I said it but hear me out. Your experiences, skills and strengths are not only about you. All of the wonderful skills you own will impact the people around you. Definitely continue to learn about and grow your skills for yourself but know there are so many others who are waiting for what you can contribute as well!

*What development session will you **attend** next?*

I love going to different development sessions. I learn something new at each session I visit, whether it's how to do a process differently or an introduction to a new tool to apply in business. I've also attended a few sessions I didn't enjoy, but that is where I've learned what NOT to do in my professional career. What development session have *you* attended lately? What did you learn that you can take back to your career environment to make things better for both you and those you work with?

*You can do this, after you **step away**.*

When the day gets hard, step away, think it through and get back on the success path. This may not be the time to act quickly. It is better to step away, meaning go to a local café or eat lunch offsite or go to a different room and breathe. Physically distance yourself from the situation. After you've had a cup of hot tea or healthy lunch or meditated into a state of calm, begin thinking about the best next step in this situation. You really can do this.

*Don't be a **corporate carbon copy**.*

Hopefully you're building great relationships with successful movers and shakers in the career you're interested in. As you're learning from them, think of ways you can continue to grow further without being just like them. As a matter of fact, forget about being just like everyone else. Get excited about what you're learning from others and how you can tweak these techniques to work for you and your ideal career. I'm excited to see what you bring. I hope you are too!

*Let me **see you**.*

If you're not visible and you're not vocal, assumptions can be made about who you are and what you're capable of in your career. Be vocal and visible, the right way, so your integrity and skills are apparent. Also, when you let people know about what you can do, it builds your brand and clearly allows people to recognize who to go to when they need what you offer. ~~Let me~~ (scratch that) Let *all* of us see you! Show us the astonishing you!

You have more influence *than you think.*

The things you do and say influence everything around you. Your contributions to your team and your goals have more impact then you will likely ever see. Keep the things you do positive and valuable for yourself and everyone around you. Be grateful and visibly accepting when people thank you or say something great about your contributions. Write down what they've said or what you've done on paper or record these positive moments on your digital device. Recognize and be proud of your influence and the contributions you make.

Be the first to **believe in you**.

Right when you're given a new role or even extended an offer on the new role, be the first to believe in you. You can do this! Know immediately that you have what it takes to help the business meet or exceed its goals. If you're staying in the same role but will change the project you're working on in your role or your own business, believe you can exceed expectations.

Action *is essential.*

In your mind, you've thought about taking action. Now is the time to do it. Don't think you need more, more, more and more before you even get started. Go ahead and take action. I speak from experience and often have to remind even myself, "Do it, Hope!" Send that email. Organize all the data. Call those marketing professionals. Whatever it is that you know needs to be done, don't procrastinate, act now.

*Maintain your courage and **keep growing** your abilities.*

Easier said than done, I know. Know that we have all at some point or another, felt discouraged in some type of career or business endeavor. We've also discovered during these experiences that we should do what we can to maintain our courage to keep moving forward and growing our abilities. Remember to go to what motivates you whether it's your Higher Power, people, songs, good photo memories or even videos, and be encouraged to use and grow the skill that's especially yours.

Take control.

You have what it takes to catapult your career. Actually, you should own your career development. Though you should certainly accept the help of great professionals, you should still own your career journey. That includes proactively seeking out beneficial development programs, networking with influential leaders and viewing failures as a path to growth.

Don't try to *do this alone*.

You don't *have* to do this alone. Actually, having the support of others will help you. Others can share ideas that you may have otherwise not known about or would have taken years to figure out. Partner with those you trust and can benefit from. Partnerships can get you even closer to the level of success you're aiming towards.

Don't be stuck *in a place that's not for you.*

Ultimately, it's up to you to decide how and where you want to move in your career. If you haven't already, discover your purpose and how you can use it for yourself and others. Staying on a career path because others think you should be there when you know it will not grow you or your purpose is not the answer. Get out of the stuck position and strategically move toward where you want and need to be.

Know your expectations and **surpass them.**

Today, take the time to write down all that is expected of you. Keep the description short. Include feedback you've been given by your leaders. Now jot down how you have fulfilled or exceeded these expectations. If you don't know your expectations, ask. If you haven't quite met those expectations, write down how and when you will. This way you're keeping yourself accountable to your next steps and hopefully excited about what you're about to accomplish.

Meet some ***incredible people*** today.

Challenge! Who is one of the most incredible people living in your industry? Think really big. Got the name? Get ready to contact this person. (Make sure this is a person you admire.) Type up a short message (2-3 sentences) that you want to send to this incredible person. Include ONE ask for them. For example, ask for a specific piece of advice or opportunity. Think positively about the response you will receive. You may be surprised.

Oopsie*! You made a mistake.*

Mistakes don't have to negatively impact your entire career. The first thing to do is acknowledge that you've made a mistake. Apologize to the people you need to give an apology. Make sure you tell them how you will make it right, what you have learned from the mistake, and how those lessons will impact your future handling of similar situations.

*Make **the good stuff** better.*

If you're looking for ways to make your work environment better, start by looking at what's already good. Think of ways to make what's good, even better. Create an intentional career environment, whether it's the culture, the processes or even the aesthetics. When choosing what to make better, consider what would make your career journey more meaningful, especially if your enhancements are aligned with your career purpose.

*Learn more about **your own** strengths.*

Learn more about your specific strengths and how you can use them. Get creative and think of out of the box, no-way-is-that-possible ideas. When thinking of how to use your ideas, don't let anything restrict you. Not time. Not money. Not logic. In the end, you may discover these creative ways to use your strengths are not that farfetched after all.

*Meet **someone new** in your career.*

For many of us, the idea of consistently meeting new people is traumatic. For others, it's exciting. No matter which group you fit into, meeting new people can become something you enjoy the more you engage in the practice. Start by meeting someone in the same role then move to meeting people with greater experience and influence in the role you're interested. If you need tips on how to initiate a meeting, ask your mentor, friends, or your career coach. You'll be glad you did!

Leave the right way.

Always leave with a visible, positive and professional impression. But I bet you knew that. How you leave will determine how you will re-enter the workforce. Huh? What you must remember is the future is not entirely predictable. For example, the people who you work with now may also be in the next line of business you go to in the future. If you leave with a great impression, and one of integrity, you'll have a better chance of entering the next business on an admirable note.

Show them.

It's true. Actions speak louder than words. Show them, whether "them" refers to your employer or your clients, you have what it takes to make the desired business goal possible. Not sure how? This is where your empowering friends, people you've networked with and knowledgeable coaches can help. Be clear of what they expect from you. Visualize it for yourself. Now show them what you can do!

Move from **OMG** *to,* "**What now?**"

Yep. That happened, but don't let it stop you from moving forward. Think about how you can make things better. Use EQ skills. These are the skills you can use to not only readjust yourself, but also to recognize and respond to the emotions of others. What do you need? What do others need in this situation in order to move forward? From there, make the right change happen.

This year loves you.

I believe "The Secret" by Rhonda Byrne. Don't know what it is? Check out the book. It's a great read. Believe in you and your dreams. See it. Speak it. Receive it. This year loves you. This year loves you. This year loves you. I can't wait to hear how this year shows its love to you! Share the news with us and celebrate!

Be in love with yourself.

Be in love with yourself. Believe it or not, it's not a bad move. It means you recognize your value and the gifts your Higher Power has given you. It means you trust your capabilities. It means you admire your integrity. It means you know you're the type of person who is genuine in their customer service. It means you build to grow. It means you are a pretty amazing person.

Abundance

Visualize you have a large amount of everything you need to be successful. With no restrictions, imagine you have the support you need, the finances you need, the coaching you need, and the mentors you need to make things happen beyond what you could ever see. Imagine receiving your career endeavors in abundance. Keep that visualization at the top of your mind all day, then receive it all.

Revamp your strategy.

Doing the same thing all the time and still not meeting your career goals may mean you need to revamp your strategy. To revamp means you change the structure of your career goal. For example, revamp your strategy of sending a bunch of resumes to different companies to networking with employees who actually work with your ideal employers.

Things aren't just changing, **they're** ***accelerating****.*

You've heard for years that the industry is always changing. The catch is they're not only changing but changing fast! I challenge you to go beyond being adaptable to change. *Be the change.* Be the innovator. Be the person to courageously outrun all the great ideas the industry has now.

Don't be busy *just for the sake of being busy.*

Have you gotten busy again? Here's another reminder that being busy to show you are a hard worker may not be the best option for you. Being busy gives the impression you'll take a lot of what people give to you. This will back fire. People may think you can do a lot of work in a short amount of time, when really, you're up all night, working tons of overtime and missing a lot in your personal life to get the job done. Don't let this happen to you. Remember your career purpose and the brand you want to make clear. Align that with what you do.

*Have **faith**.*

Faith. "The substance of things hoped for." Hope, "to expect with confidence." Have faith and hope when pursuing your career endeavors. Either way you position it, it is all about belief. Have faith—believe that you are capable and you will see your career dreams a reality.

*Make it **easy** for the interviewer.*

Interviews work both ways. The interviewer wants to hire the right candidate and the candidate wants to have the best chance at securing a desired role. Now imagine an interviewer who has been talking to people all day for the same role. Better yet, the interviewer has you as the first interviewee, but is thinking about all the other candidates she will have to interview after you. When you walk in for your interview, make it easy for the interviewer to see what you offer with your drive, your skill, and relative experience in a way that she will remember.

Showing your value is not arrogant, it's ***necessary****.*

Telling people what you offer gives them the gift of knowing where to go if they need the skill you have. Otherwise, hiding your gift or keeping it a secret keeps everyone in the dark. Tell people about your gift. Clearly show them the skillset you have. Do this in a way that will show them you're there to help by offering them a solution. This is not arrogant. It's necessary for the growth of yourself, your team, your organization, and your profession.

*Don't put off "**doing it BIG**" until tomorrow.*

Do it BIG today. Give your all with what you have and with what you can imagine now. Your industry and all of the individuals who work for the industry and those who enjoy the products of the industry are waiting for your BIG ideas. Do it BIG today. Worry less about perfection because you'll do it better tomorrow.

Make it *a fantastic day!*

I know I told you before, but I have to say this one again. It wasn't until someone told me to MAKE it a fantastic day that I realized creating that greatness was mostly *my* responsibility. It wasn't something I should just expect to happen, instead *I* could be the person that makes fantastic things happen that day. You are too. How exciting! When you walk through those business doors or log onto your computer to do business, MAKE it a fantastic day!

Surround *yourself with greatness.*

Surrounding yourself with great people, great experiences, and great environments will take you a super long way. You know that, right? Accept that being surrounded by greatness will inspire, motivate, bring out creativity, and initiate the new. Don't be afraid or nervous about that. Go for it. Make it a mission to be around greatness, even people and things that are greater than you.

*Be **better today** than you were yesterday.*

You have accomplished so much, and you should be proud of this. Celebrate on your terms. Take a moment to enjoy the recognition. Then take time to think about how you can make things even better. Perhaps it is using the same technique you utilized before, or it could be a totally new idea. Either way, have fun contemplating ways to make career better.

Aim *higher.*

According to the Webster dictionary, one definition describes **faith** as "something that is believed especially with strong conviction." Do you have faith? Then practice it. Believe in big moves you can make in your career. The more you believe it, the more likely you are to find ways to aim higher and achieve your career goals.

Don't give up *on meeting your professional goals.*

I have been there. You know. That place where you tried and didn't get what you wanted. I've even been in that place where you thought you were doing great, only to be told you're not. What I've learned through these experiences is if this is where the process has put you, you belong there—and for your own *good*. It took a former colleague to remind me of that, so I never gave up. Now it's my turn to remind you. Don't give up on meeting your professional goals.

Reflect *on your professional progress.*

There are so many reasons to look back at all of the things you've accomplished. There are so many reasons to document your journey. Buy your favorite notebook or purchase a cool binder. This is the place you'll jot down or document your accomplishments. Unlike the previous tip I gave you, also document your failures and how you navigated them. Write down cool stuff you've done too. Slip in the rewards you've gotten. Now take a look at your progress. You'll notice some things you've never considered before. Some practices you'll want to continue doing and there are some you'll want to stop. You'll see yourself in a whole new way, including how far you have come!

Remember ***your manifesto***.

It all started when one of my coaches asked me to write my manifesto. She explained this involved writing who I **know** I am. This has been one of the most meaningful experiences in my career. If you've been to one of my coaching sessions, you know I've asked you about your own manifesto. What do you *know* you are destined to do? Write it down as a simple sentence and put it in an attractive place that makes you smile when you see it every day.

*Who's **the person** you want to meet?*

I'm sure there is someone in your life you'd love to meet. What are they like? Why do you want to meet them? What is it you can gain from them? What is it they can gain from you? If you're driving, be sure to write your answers down in your favorite notebook when it's safe. If you're still, write it down now. Answers to these questions will set you up for success, especially if the person you want to meet asks you, "What can I do for you?"

When the right door of opportunity opens,
GO*!!!*

You've been working for this moment for quite some time. You've been on the lookout for the ideal career opportunity and now it's looking you in your face. Go for it! Don't let procrastination mess things up for you. Don't let fear force you to freeze up. Believe in yourself and your capabilities and go for that opportunity you've been preparing to grab.

*Don't waste **your time** doing everything.*

Hard for some of us to swallow, I know. Don't waste your time trying to do *every single thing*. Instead, excel at what you are purposed to do. Because you know yourself, your purpose and your matching strengths by now, focus on building that version of you. This is where you'll find the most success and fulfillment.

Enjoy *what you do every day.*

Operating in your purpose throughout your career will bring you fulfillment. But what about the times you find yourself in another position until your ideal career is made available to you? Glad you asked. Make that "in-the-meantime-position" one you can enjoy. I speak from experience that there are things you can do to make the position meaningful, goal-oriented, enjoyable, and of course, purposeful.

Start *now.*

Life gets in the way for us all, but that's when we have to come back to our favorite place and reprioritize. Think about what's important and what's really stopping you from moving forward. Now, stop waiting. Start moving forward.

*Do **more** than exist.*

You're nice. You're professional. You complete your work on time. You do what is in the job description. Hey! Don't just exist. Do more than exist. Add a lil' spice to your business day. Stand out.

Attitudes *make a huge difference.*

Yep. Here's the attitude thing again. As you aim to move in your career, know your attitude plays a big part. Know that people hire professionals they want to be around. Your daily attitude speaks about your integrity and the likelihood others want to be around you. Read more about emotional intelligence and how you can grow your EQ for yourself and those you work with every day.

Become *your full potential.*

One day, I had to pause and ask myself if I was really operating in my full potential. Was I giving my best in what I do? Was I growing my purpose/strength? I'm glad I reflected on my answers to those questions. I became a better person for doing the personal background check. I challenge you to do the same. Remind yourself what your full potential is, trust your capabilities, and become the full you.

Every step counts.

Big or small, every step you make counts. The important part is that you take that step. Not later, but now. You will look back and appreciate the positive move forward that you made back then. If it's a little step, take it. If it's a huge, positive step, take it. Recruit great supporters along the way and enjoy the journey.

If the wall is in front of you, **maneuver**.

Don't give up. You may just need to change your path. The new path you take could be left, right, under or even over the wall. Better yet, create your own window or door in the wall. Examine the situation and be okay with making a different move. How will you maneuver today?

*Your personal development is **in your hands**.*

Take responsibility for your own personal development. Own it. Be proactive. You have what it takes to genuinely connect with people who can teach you more. You have access to tools, such as online research engines that can lead you to new learning places. Use your voice to ask your leaders about training tools and other advancement opportunities available at your organization.

*You are **not alone**.*

Come on. You've read this before. You are not alone, and you absolutely shouldn't be. As you navigate through your career, avoid going at it alone. Consider the feedback and tips from others. Engage in sharing opportunities where you can help others all while learning in the process. AND don't hesitate to ask the right people to help you too. You'll be surprised by the responses you get from people who would love to help you.

Be committed to growing.

Know the world around you is constantly growing in an effort to be more innovative. The world and all the ecosystems involved want to be better at the services they provide to each of us and the products they market. You should be growing too. In an effort to become better and better, commit to growing in the most enjoyable way possible, whether that's through coaching, free videos, conferences, or networks. Stay committed to growing. Be a part of the innovative growth opportunities that world is affording us.

*Your professional strength **builds all** of us.*

Know that using your professional strengths is not just about you. It is about all the people you are destined to touch. It's about simultaneously seeking and being the resource for growth. Your strengths have the capacity to help all of us grow in our own personal and career endeavors. For that, thank you for sharing what you have. Always know that we are grateful.

*Keep it **simple**.*

When determining how to reach your career goals, keep it simple. Don't overthink it. Don't make it complicated. Don't create a long and drawn out plan. Keep it simple. Keeping it simple will benefit everyone involved and it's likely to be more enjoyable as you go through this goal-catching journey.

*Send a **message** to your favorite role model.*

Take the risk and send a nice, short, message to your favorite role model, no matter how corny you think it is. Let them know how much you admire them. Let them know exactly what it is that you admire about them and what difference they've made for you. Don't expect a reply, just know that you've done a HUGE thing. You've put a big smile on someone's face!

Your own ***definition*** *of success matters.*

We know how the dictionary defines success. And that's important. You should know how *your business* defines success. And that's important too. More importantly, know what success looks like for you personally. In other words, define success for yourself.

*Can you **see it**?*

I imagine I've given you enough healthy nudges. Okay, hopefully you've discovered your purpose by now. If so, you've decided what you will do. You even <u>said</u> your use of your purpose will have a positive influence on many people. But have you visualized that yet? Take a moment. Visualize how your purpose will make a positive impact on the people you intend to touch. See that? Now go for it!

*Your goals are **possible**.*

Because you are here, because you have the ideas, because you've been working on growing you – your goal is possible.
Believe in all that you are and all that you're purposed to do. Believe that your professional goals are possible. Connect with the right people and the right tools and keep your eye on the possibilities.

Thank your Higher Power.

Through all of your endeavors, have you thanked your Higher Power lately? Don't get so busy that you forget the most important item on your list—your Higher Power. Today, focus on giving thanks for all that you have and all that you will gain in the future. Consistent gratitude will take you a long way in your career…and life.

Recognize **your peaceful, motivational place**.

It's time to go out and explore. Explore new rooms. Check out open houses. Take a hike. Check out new bookstores. Take note of what places make you feel good. Now make that space yours whether it's outdoors, on your desk or in a special place in your home. I've done this myself, and I must say, there's nothing like a place you know you can go to for peace and career motivation.

Treat yourself today!

Life happens, but have you taken the time to treat yourself? You should. No career to-do's today. Treat yourself with something you personally enjoy. Maybe it's an extra hour of sleep. Maybe it's a chocolate shake. Maybe it's time to read a good book. It could even be cooking something healthy. Whatever it is, grab positive energy and treat yourself to something that makes you smile today.

Help them.

You have grown so much and have many experiences worth sharing. So many people have helped you, seen and unseen. Today, find a way to give back to someone else in a way that feels good to you. Even better, help them with the skill and purpose given to you.

Grow your *Emotional Intelligence* *(EQ)*.

It's true. You can grow your EQ. No matter what your current EQ, you can grow it even more. Do just that. I encourage you to focus on the self-awareness category. It will get you far in your professional role and career communications. Try using free and credible websites to learn more. Need help finding these sites? Connect with us on social media to find others who are already building their EQ skills.

*Don't **overwhelm** yourself.*

There comes a time when you want to do so much to grow. There may even be a time when you think you HAVE to do so much to grow. Don't overwhelm yourself. Keep your growth simple. Visualize where you want to be. Write it down and don't over embellish. Now claim it. Make it happen. Remember, none of the successful kingdoms were built in a day.

Follow up.

Follow up with a professional you've met within the past 6 months. Keep your follow up communication short. For example, drop them a three-sentence email or send them a card to let them know you're using specific advice they've given you. This expresses that you appreciated meeting them and valued their insight. This also keeps the professional relationship growing further.

Be aware *of what makes you happy.*

One of the best ways to find out what you want to do in your career is to recognize the moments at work that make you happy. What topic in the meeting perked your interest? What projects lit your fire? Consider paying attention to what lights you up for the next two weeks and write it down every time you sense it. You may be surprised at what you discover.

Winning *is an EVERYDAY accomplishment.*

You win whenever you give it your best shot! You win when you go for that project or new role, even though you're super scared. You win when you help another teammate with a goal he or she struggles with, but that you find extra easy. Embrace your wins, big or small, write them down in your journal or even email yourself. You'll thank me for this later.

*Networking **should be** building relationships*

I look at networking in a very different way than some. Networking is important, but it's not about checking people off your "to-meet" list. Instead, networking works best when it's viewed as building relationships as you meet new influential people. Keep in contact. Receive their recommendations and give back in the best way you can. Use the page over there to write down their names and contact info as you go. Oh, and have fun with the people you meet. You'll find that relationships, not just networking, are the electric source for the career builder.

*Know where to **find your ammo**.*

There have been many days I lost my motivation. I just couldn't get back on the journey to run with my ideas or even use my God-given purpose. When this happens, I have to re-engage my professional ammo. My professional ammo is watching an educational video or listening to an audio book or bouncing ideas off my friends or seeing others grow in their careers. What's your professional ammo? Use that resource whenever you think you're losing your motivation.

What in the world is the benefit of **having a coach**?

Like coaches in sports, coaches can be your third eye. Your sideline or balcony perspective giver. This is the person you want to connect with when you can't seem to get beyond a wall even when you believe you've tried everything possible. Hey, you may have tried everything possible yourself, however it doesn't hurt to have another person evaluate the details and recommend a new play that you may not have considered. Get a coach and link up with them at a time and cadence that fits you both.

*There is **no end goal** in a purposeful career journey.*

Development in your career never stops, and that's a good thing. Keep learning new skills that will help you achieve. Even if you see yourself at the finish line and only want to retire and go on a forever vacation, there is still an opportunity to explore new ideas and tools that you can share with up and coming newbies.

Know ***your role*** AND ***your business***.

Knowing your role expectations and the goal of the business will help you navigate to your ideal career. Take time today to really understand your role, even outside of what's written on paper. Ask your leaders and read public business papers to get perspective. You just might have an "aha" moment leading you to the next big move.

*The story doesn't end **until you say** it does.*

You have the opportunity to end the story how you best see fit. This includes a layoff or even getting fired. Don't end the story with anger and sadness, though those are valid feelings to have. End your story in a positive way by taking what you've learned or relationships you've built to a greater path. Then start the next "book" the way you want it to start.

*You have **the unique gift** we're waiting for.*

Like most of us, you may have the feeling you have to be quiet about your accomplishments. Or you may be so busy trying to get the work done, that you simply don't think about sharing what you're doing. Even worse, you may not be using your gift. Remember, so many people are waiting for you to use your gift and make it known to the world. Let us know. Don't just show us your gift, tell us about it. This way we can celebrate with you AND know just where to go should we need your skill. We're waiting.

Really? **Why not?**

What? You're not going take the career change you were looking for? You don't think you're (insert word here) enough to go for the role you want? Ask yourself *why* you think this way over and over again. Get to the root of your hesitation. You may just find the risk you thought was too big to take won't break you.

*Wait until you **hear the real** story.*

There are so many assumptions that can be made about what colleagues and leaders have done or thought. Don't fall into the gossip trap. Don't make assumptions about what you've heard or seen. This will take you to a negative place mentally that will impede your journey. First ask yourself if the gossip is important for you to know and why. If it is, go to the right source and ask questions or for support.

*Your Higher Power is **bigger than that**. Yep, even bigger than that.*

If you're wondering if there is any way in the world your dreams can happen, yes, they can. It may or may not turn out the way you intended. Sometimes it's even better than you imagined. What's even more important is knowing the source that grants you your dreams. Your Higher Power. Your Universe. Your Alpha and Omega. Your God. The source of your strength is indeed bigger than you know and delivers possibilities bigger than you knew could even exist. I know, because my Higher Power has proven to be bigger to me many, many times.

*Your favorite **color** belongs there.*

You didn't expect this one, I know, but hear me out. I love wearing my favorite color that others find attractive for my complexion. I love painting my favorite color (which is a totally different color) on the walls of my home. It's something about wearing your favorite that gives you energy and confidence to move forward during your workday. Having your favorite color in your home gives you the comfort you need to rest or sparks of creativeness when coming up with new ideas for your career. Find your color if you haven't already and use it to find your muse or comfort zone.

Do **what you said** *you'd do. Today.*

You said you were going to apply for that role. You said you were going to get that certification. You said you were going to build a business of your own. You said you were going to implement that new business idea. Go for it. Talk is cheap. The great thing you said you were going to do, do it and start today.

*What are you **grateful** for today?*

Now's a time to appreciate what you have *now*. Actually, every morning is a great time for reflection. As a matter of fact, every morning, I take a moment to say what I'm grateful for. If you were a fly on the wall, you may hear me say I'm grateful for the birds singing to me before I start my career endeavors for the day. On another day, you may hear me say I'm grateful for my health. This routine gives me a great view on life. You should try it too. What are you grateful for today?

You were **created by magnificence**
to be magnificent.

Have complete faith in your capabilities. Feel confident about and be driven to grow your purpose and career strengths. Know that you were created by an incredible Power. Know you were born by a family who hoped you'd have a positive influence on all the people around you. Don't question who you have in your corner. Go for your goal knowing you not only have a reason to, but you have the backing to make it happen.

*If you took a **snapshot**, what would it look like?*

Taking a simple snapshot of the career opportunity you're going for helps get the juices flowing about how to get where you want to go. What's a snapshot? I'm glad you asked. A snapshot, in this instance, is a picture or a description of the role you want. Make sure it's a quick view. Try pulling a view from a magazine or writing a description on an index card. Once you do, take a look at it and come up with ideas on how you can grab what you see.

*You are the **future workforce**. What does that look like?*

No matter your age, or your level of experience, you are what the future workforce looks like. Professional environments are always changing. Take time today to visualize what the future workforce will provide as well as what it will need. What positive impact for the future workforce will you provide? Now figure out how you will engage that impact in the workforce of the future.

*Bring **your own chair** to the room.*

One of the most endearing workshop ideas I had was bringing your own seat to the decision table. During this workshop, my attendees were encouraged to actually bring their OWN chairs in the room. Not only was it fun, but the symbolic meaning behind it was super impactful. Don't just take a seat at the table, bring your own seat to the table. Make your presence and ideas known by feeling empowered enough to bring your best self holistically. Your presence AND your own seat that you feel comfortable in whether symbolic or not will make the difference.

***Diversify* your mind and *your decisions*.**

We've all heard the saying, "If it ain't broke, don't fix it." Now hear, "Even if it ain't broke, make it better and better." Avoid thinking the same way and making the same decisions. Always be open to diversifying your thoughts from only systematic or even only analytical perspectives. Use a more skillful way to expand your thoughts and your professional strengths.

Accountability

Know what keeps you accountable to your goals, your dreams, and your vision for yourself? If you don't, now is a great time to realize something that keeps you on task as it relates to your professional journey. Whatever that is, it is what will keep you responsible and straight forward. Be accountable to all the career aspirations you have. This will prove your commitment.

*What does your **circle of diversity** look like?*

Today, take a look at all of the individuals who support you. Are they the same? Do they all agree with all of your choices? Do they all give you the same ideas? If the answer is yes to any of these questions, it's time to diversify your circle. Meet individuals with new ideas, different perspectives, and varied experiences. Dare to be challenged. Make a list, right here on the page, of individuals that come to mind. Then take some time to meet with them.

*Know where to get **your fresh air**.*

Don't keep working for the sake of working. Don't continue be involved in various work groups because you believe that is the right thing to do. Don't stress out so much that you harm your wellbeing. Recognize when you have had enough and go get some fresh air; whether you literally go outside to get fresh air or figuratively do something else that keeps you refreshed.

List your **real investors**.

Get ready to make a list of all of the influential people who have clearly invested in your career, large or small. Today, take a page from your notebook, an index card from your studies or even a sticky note from your desk and jot down all of their names. Now reconnect with each one of them by sending a short email, letter, or text. This will help you continue to build relationships with influential professionals already in your corner. It also demonstrates you're not always reaching out only when you need something. Now keep the list handy.

Update *your priority list.*

List everything you want to do to improve your career. Then put all the lists in order of what is important to you. Start with what matters the most to you. Only include to-do's that will actually impact your career journey. Throw away items on the list that don't align with where you're trying to go. This exercise will make it much clearer and easier to reach your goal.

It's as simple as that.

The best managers display the best leadership skills. The worst managers have the worst leadership skills. The best leadership skills are not all about doing excellent tactical work, it's more about influence and servitude. If you are looking to have a leadership role, whether laterally or vertically, learn more about positively impacting and serving people.

*"**Thank-you**" can be a life saver.*

By now I hope you remembered to say "thank you" this morning. Now remember to say "thank you" to people who made a positive impact on your career journey whether that's a leader, peer, or friend. Today, send them a note, letter, text, email, or an extra cool gift if you can. Remember, this is not just a follow up note. This should specifically thank them for the particular nugget of truth, wisdom, opportunity, or advice they've given you. This means a lot to them and in the end, will mean a lot to you.

See yourself as others see you.

Be brave and take a look at yourself through the lens of others. Wait, hear me out. Of course, you can get feedback from an official 360 assessment, like I did. Though it is a wonderful tool, there is an easier way to gain an honest snapshot of your brand. Ask your friends. Ask your family. Ask you colleagues to tell you the one word that describes you. Once you do this, take a look at all the words to see if you need to promote a stronger image or an image with greater consistency.

Identify ***the difference***.

I never knew one of the coolest things I would learn is to determine what item in the lineup was different from the rest. In school, I had to learn which one of those items were not the same as the others. Even while watching television, I sang songs about an item in a group that was not like the others. At least one was indeed different. Who is different from you? How are they different? What is it that makes that person a more successful professional than those less successful? I do this often with hopes of learning something new from all of those who have been successful in their careers. I'm grateful for the nuggets (from others' successes) provide me.

Write it down.

You've heard if from your friends. You've read it in the Scriptures. You should give it a try because you'll be grateful for what this assignment brings to you. Whatever your career goals are don't simply think about it, write it down. If you want, expand on it in detail. Want to go even farther? Post it on your wall, make it a screen saver or clip it to your vision board. See it every day and watch how it motivates and guides you.

*Get **beyond** what's not in your job description.*

Get over "that's not in my job description." Avoid only sticking to what you see in black and white as your job description. What I've found in my career journey is stepping beyond what my job describes not just in any way, but in an intentional way that brings me greater success and recognition than just checking off boxes in a job description. See how else you can add value to your career role and choose to add that additional thing **if it works for you and accommodates your career goal**.

*Give feedback the **gift of perspective**.*

Positive feedback can be super easy to receive. Critical feedback, on the hand, can be challenging, especially when you don't agree with the feedback given. Consider this, you do not always have control over the feedback you will and will not receive. While you celebrate exciting feedback, consider being open to relevant critical feedback. Whether true or not, they give the opportunity to put something into perspective and to acknowledge the perspective of others. After reviewing, if it does absolutely nothing for you, throw it away and forget about it.

*Think **unlimited** growth.*

How big are you thinking? Think bigger. Make your thoughts limitless. Imagine monumental career positions and growth opportunities that you can achieve. Think about big crowds of customers you can positively touch. Think about unlimited ways you can influence business growth. Thinking bigger helps you see chances you may have otherwise missed.

Meet ***your accountability buddy****.*

Once you set your career goals, you should be held accountable. Wait. Who is it that keeps you accountable? Don't hesitate to meet with that trusted supporter, an accountability buddy, or coach to track your word and keep you on the right path to achieve your goals.

Teach them who you are.

Don't assume business professionals will know who you are and the skills you bring. Teach them who you are. This means being consistent with how you describe yourself and the professional image you present. Start with the signature in your emails and speaking up during meetings about areas you are strong in or have ideas about. Remember though, don't brag while doing so, instead humbly express to others the expertise you can offer on the topic.

Run *that thing.*

Being put in a place to lead an initiative or a team can be intimidating, especially for the first time. Confidently know that you've been given that opportunity for a reason. Someone believes in you and your Higher Power has all the equipment and tools you need. Feel empowered by the opportunity and run that thing!

Own it.

When you know you've made a career mistake, own it. Don't try to forget it and definitely don't just avoid it. Own the mistake by acknowledging what was done. Just as important, tell what you've learned and what you will do to avoid the mistake going forward. This will give you and others peace of mind, a new reason to respect you, and a cartload of integrity.

*It actually may be **okay** to take the risk.*

You'll often never know how far you can stretch and how much you can actually achieve until you take the risk. Risk doesn't have to be a scary word or an all-the-time task. Instead of intimidating yourself with long lists of why you should or shouldn't take a risk, understand what you are actually risking. What you will see is that some things on your "risk list" is not scary at all, but fantastic opportunities.

It's going to take **more than just one** *great resume.*

It's smart to invest in improving your resume. However, practicing your interview techniques are great investments too. It's also wise to invest in your public brand and your relationships before the professional opening is ever posted. Seek a proven professional coach today to help engage all the tools needed to set the stage for your next career move.

*Do **today** what you will later wish you did yesterday.*

The moments in time I regret most is when I waited to execute important goals or steps in the direction of my dreams. Part of it was my desire to gain approval first. Part of it was my desire to achieve perfection before I moved forward. I often failed to listen to my intuition and sometimes fell astray from exercising my faith. Those moments would have been easier if I hadn't hesitated. Learn from my errors. Trust your intuition. Sometimes your hopes manifest when you simply move today.

Tell them ***what you forgot***.

Congratulations! You had a great interview, but there's something you forgot to tell them.

OR the networking moment you had was actually fun, but you forgot to say something you really wish you had.

Don't worry. Create a second chance. It's always a great idea to follow up with a kind note of appreciation that includes what you forgot to mention during the interview. For example, *"Thank you for taking the time to meet with me. I really enjoyed our conversation. I also wanted to let you know…"*

*Use your "**let's get pumped**" move.*

Nervous about the next business move you'll make? We have all felt that nervousness. What will help propel you is doing your "let's get pumped" move! Think about what is it that gets you more excited and less nervous about making big moves. Is it raising your hands? Is it loudly singing and dancing to your favorite song? Is it shaking your wrists? Is it giving thanks? Is it getting a supportive hug from a loved one? Whatever it is, use that positive energy to help you make your next business move.

Bless someone today.

The thing about having a wonderfully-given purpose is there is a specific reason it was given to you. Speaking professionally, use your purposed gift to bless others as you have been admonished to do so. What I mean is don't just bless everyone with everything you have in only a spiritual building. During your workday, use your purposed gift intentionally the way your Higher Power has instructed in your work environment too.

Ask for help.

You are amazing and the skill you have is phenomenal. Imagine how much better your results can be when you seek help. Feel good about asking for help from both supportive and successful individuals. Ask your friends for help. Ask your family for help. Ask colleagues for help. Ask your leaders for help. Reach out and be overjoyed by the results.

*Always **count** your blessings.*

Count your blessings in your current profession. This includes the health benefits you receive, reimbursements, retirement match, people, and growth opportunities. Either you'll be reminded just how great your current opportunity is OR you'll be well prepared for negotiations during your next career offer.

Make ***time for what matters***.

I used to work long hours to gain both notoriety and money. One day I realized while I was making all that money, I wasn't taking the time to spend it. I also realized I looked a mess after all that work. Even more so, I wasn't spending time with my family and friends. Here is where learned I need to make time for what matters. I encourage you to do the same.

*Learn **something new** today.*

There is nothing like learning something new and fascinating, especially if it will enhance your life or career. Take the time to learn something new today. Look for affordable conferences nearby, buy a book on an intriguing topic, or read fresh magazine articles. You'll certainly reap the benefits when you work on that next project.

Be filled.

Purpose is what helps you feel fulfilled in your career. For example, there's nothing worse than going to work every day and dreading every moment of it even before you get there because you aren't operating in your purpose. Find your purpose in your career. Why are you there? Find your purpose where you are now and how you can use it so you will be fully used *and* fully filled.

Every **now and then we need extra inspiration.**

Every now and then, we all need inspiration OR <u>extra</u> inspiration. I'm glad you're here. I hope this book gives you the inspiration you need to keep moving forward. Better yet, I hope the words in this book give you what you need to be successful. However, every now and then, we need different types of inspiration. Today, figure out what inspires you, whether it be videos, written words, movies, pets, or support of a loved one, and use it to help give you the fuel you need to keep engaging in your career endeavors.

ABOUT THE AUTHOR

Hope LeNoir is an award winning and internationally read author, an expert Career Coach with results, and a well-known inspirational speaker. She is also the owner of Rise and Fly LLC, whose purpose is to help professionals advance their performance and their career journey. Her specialty is uniting career purpose with spiritual purpose.

ADDITIONAL BOOKS

RUSH: Embracing your purpose and all of the psychological thrillers it brings with it
By Hope LeNoir

7 Women 7 Words: A collection of inspirational essays
By Dianne L. Malone, Hope LeNoir, Demetria Adair, Hiedi Emily, Carmen Patton, Ciera Shannon, Rhonda Maydwell

Made in the USA
Middletown, DE
13 June 2023